The Story of the Civil War

Heroes of the Civil War

by Susan S. Wittman

CAPSTONE PRESS
a capstone imprint

Fact Finders Books are published by Capstone Press,
1710 Roe Crest Drive, North Mankato, Minnesota 56003
www.capstonepub.com

Copyright © 2015 by Capstone Press, a Capstone imprint. All rights reserved. No part of this publication may be reproduced in whole or in part, or stored in a retrieval system, or transmitted in any form or by any means, electronic, mechanical, photocopying, recording, or otherwise, without written permission of the publisher.

Library of Congress Cataloging-in-Publication Data
Wittman, Susan S.
  Heroes of the Civil War / by Susan S. Wittman.
    pages cm. — (Fact finders. The story of the Civil War)
  Includes bibliographical references and index.
  Summary: "Describes heroes of the American Civil War from both the Union and the Confederacy, including battlefield heroes, political figures, and others"—Provided by publisher.
  ISBN 978-1-4914-0720-2 (library binding)
  ISBN 978-1-4914-0727-1 (paperback)
  ISBN 978-1-4914-0731-8 (ebook pdf)
1. United States—History—Civil War, 1861-1865—Biography—Juvenile literature. I. Title.
E467.K65 2015
973.7092'2—dc23 [B]   2014007634

Developed and Produced by Focus Strategic Communications, Inc.
  Adrianna Edwards: project manager
  Ron Edwards, Jessica Pegis: editors
  Rob Scanlan: designer and compositor
  Karen Hunter: media researcher
  Francine Geraci: copyeditor and proofreader
  Wendy Scavuzzo: fact checker

Photo Credits
Corbis, 5, Bettmann, 19, 25; Courtesy of the Oblate Sisters of Providence Archives, 20; Getty Images Inc: MPI, 23; National Geographic, 21; Library of Congress: Prints and Photographs Division, 9, 11, 13, 15, 17, 22, 27 (right), 28; Public Domain, 27 (left); Shutterstock: Christophe Boisson cover (bkgrnd), millennium arkay, cover

TABLE OF CONTENTS

Chapter 1	With Honor and Courage	4
Chapter 2	Courageous Leaders	8
Chapter 3	Battlefield Legends	12
Chapter 4	Lifesavers	20
Chapter 5	Citizen Heroes	24

Glossary	30
Read More	31
Critical Thinking Using the Common Core	31
Internet Sites	32
Index	32

With Honor and Courage

The Civil War (1861-1865) was the United States' bloodiest conflict. Eleven states had seceded from the Union by 1861. They formed the new Confederate States of America. Confederates believed each state should have more power. They also wanted to keep slavery because their economy depended on it.

More people lived in the Northern states. These states had more jobs and more money. This meant the Union had more power in Congress. Many Northerners did not agree with slavery and wanted it abolished.

The Union and the Confederacy could not agree. When war broke out in 1861, Union troops fought to keep the country together. Confederate troops went to war over states' rights and slavery.

secede: to withdraw formally from a group or an organization, often to form another organization

Congress: the government body of the United States that makes laws, made up of the Senate and the House of Representatives

abolish: to put an end to something officially

After four long years, the Civil War ended in 1865. Confederate General Robert E. Lee surrendered to Union General Ulysses S. Grant. The nation would remain as one.

During the hard-fought war, heroes emerged on both sides of the conflict. These brave men and women fought the Civil War on and off the battlefield.

Heroes in War

Many people acted with honor and courage to defend their beliefs during the Civil War. These people are often described as heroes. During the Civil War, they were admired for their bravery. Many risked their lives to protect others.

FAST FACTS

More than 3 million Americans fought in the Civil War. For many years historians believed that about 620,000 soldiers died in the conflict. Recently experts think the number of deaths is closer to 750,000.

The South Carolina legislature met at the Old State House in Columbia, South Carolina, to vote to leave the Union on December 20, 1860.

Major Events of the Civil War

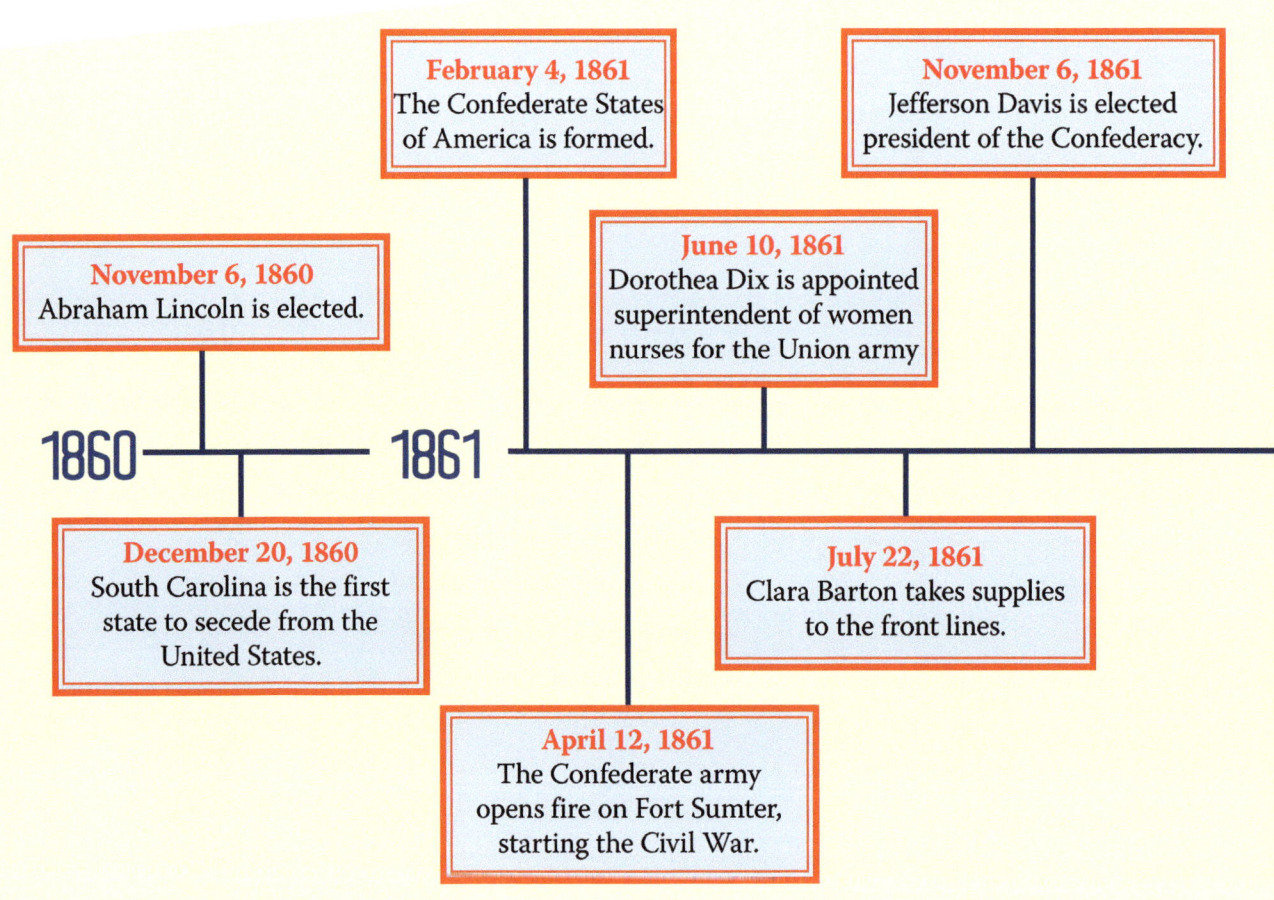

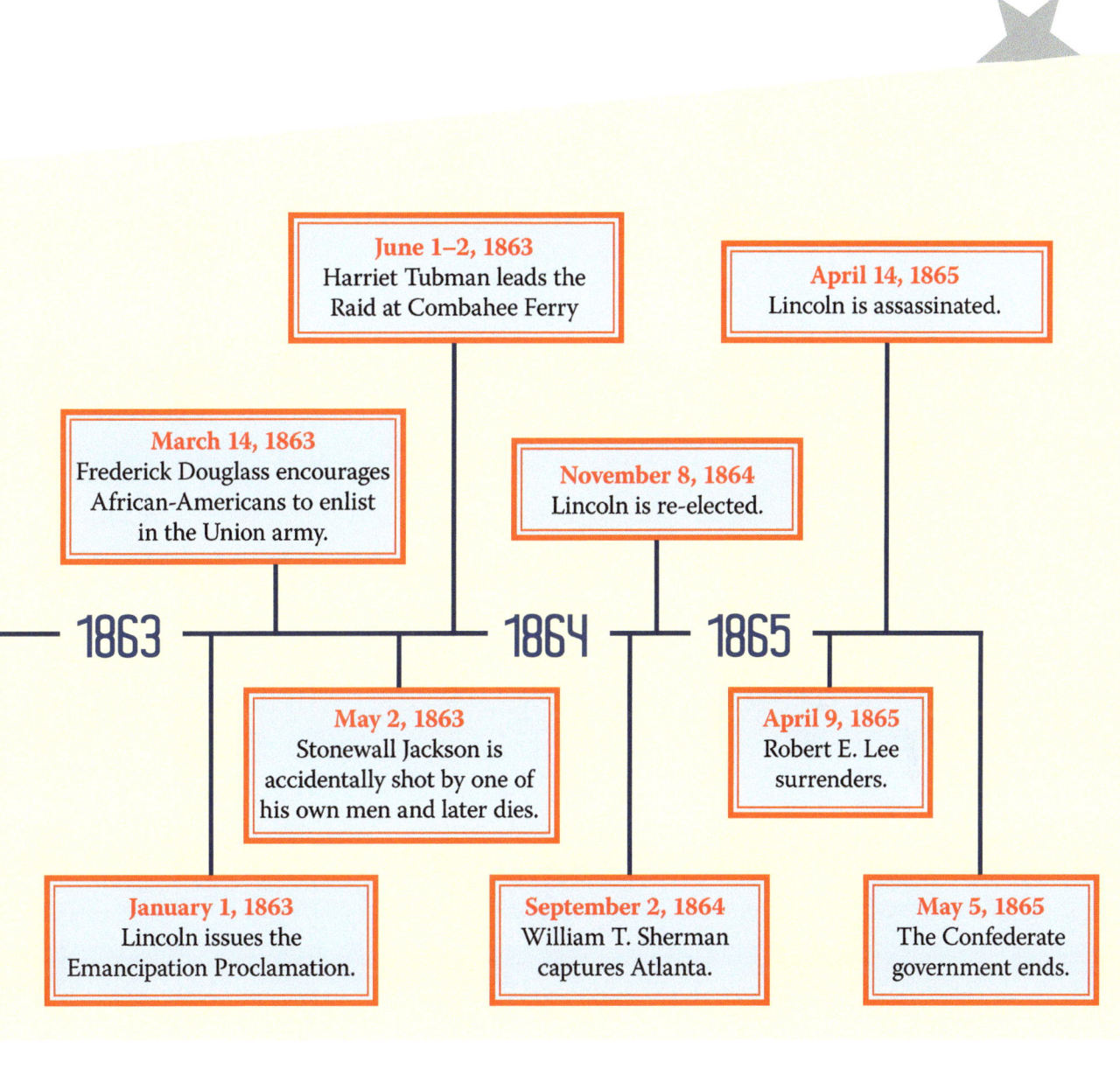

Courageous Leaders

During the Civil War, the United States was divided into two nations, each with its own leader. Abraham Lincoln became president of the United States in 1861. Confederate states were led by Jefferson Davis.

Abraham Lincoln

Lincoln was elected just before the Civil War started. By the end of the war he would be remembered as the man who kept the Union together and ended slavery.

During the war, Lincoln learned about military strategy. He worked with Union generals. The Union fought many bloody battles against the Confederates. But Lincoln knew the issue of slavery had to be settled to end the war. Five days after the Battle of Antietam, Lincoln made a presidential proclamation. He said that he would free slaves in any Confederate state that did not return to the Union by January 1, 1863. On New Year's Day, he signed the Emancipation Proclamation. This document declared that slaves in Confederate states were free. But the Confederacy did not follow Union laws.

proclamation: a public announcement or statement

emancipation: freedom from slavery or control

Abraham Lincoln, 16th president of the United States

FAST FACTS

The Emancipation Proclamation did not include all slaves. Slaves in border states had to wait three more years. In 1865 the 13th Amendment to the Constitution outlawed slavery throughout the nation.

Jefferson Davis

On November 6, 1861, Jefferson Davis became president of the Confederate States of America. Davis promised to uphold states' rights and support slavery. Davis did not want the Confederacy to be at war. However, just two months after he took office, he told the Confederacy to attack Fort Sumter. The Civil War had begun.

Davis wanted the South to govern itself. During the war, many Southerners supported him. However, he made many mistakes. He had a difficult time running his government. Though Davis' presidency was difficult, many Southerners respected him. They believed he worked to protect the Confederate States of America.

FAST FACTS

Confederate President Jefferson Davis fled Richmond, Virginia, shortly before Union troops captured the city on April 2, 1865. He was later caught by the U.S. government and served two years in prison.

Jefferson Davis, president of the Confederate states

Battlefield Legends

Ulysses S. Grant

Lincoln was impressed by General Ulysses S. Grant's intelligence and patriotism. He made Grant lieutenant general of all the U.S. armies. George Washington was the last person to hold that position. Only Lincoln had more military power.

Grant built strong relationships with his soldiers. They trusted him, and fought hard to save the Union. Grant and his soldiers chased General Robert E. Lee and his men across Virginia. Grant knew the Union had more resources than the Confederates. He encouraged his soldiers to fight with all their might. Eventually, Lee's forces were tired and outnumbered.

FAST FACTS

Grant went by many names. He was born Hiram Ulysses Grant, but his West Point application accidentally listed his name as Ulysses S. Grant. The "S" was short for his mother's maiden name, Simpson. Grant did not challenge the error.

patriotism: love for one's country

Lee surrendered on April 9, 1865, at Appomattox Courthouse, Virginia. Grant could have been tough on the Confederate troops. Instead he was generous. Confederate soldiers and officers were allowed to return to their families and homes. Grant was hailed as a hero by Northerners.

In 1869 Grant became president of the United States. He served until 1877.

Robert E. Lee

General Robert E. Lee was another talented general. He led Southern troops through fierce battles during the Civil War. Despite many victories, the fighting took its toll. The Confederates ran out of resources, including men. Lee offered to resign from the Confederate Army after their defeat at Gettysburg. But Davis would not let him. Davis believed Lee was the best man to lead Confederate troops.

Despite his best efforts Lee was forced to surrender. He felt he had no choice. After Lee signed the terms of surrender, he spoke these words to his soldiers: "Men, we have fought through the war together. I have done my best for you; my heart is too full to say more."

When Lee returned to Richmond, he was given a hero's welcome. Many people were upset the Confederacy had lost the war. But Southerners respected Lee's efforts. He encouraged Southerners to put the war behind them and work for unity.

Robert E. Lee

Thomas "Stonewall" Jackson

Confederate General Thomas "Stonewall" Jackson was known as a determined leader. Early in the war, he and his soldiers won many battles. Jackson did not live to see the end of the Civil War. He was accidentally shot by his own troops on May 2, 1863. Jackson's left arm had to be amputated. Eight days later, he died of pneumonia.

The Stone Wall

It was July 21, 1861. Union troops were winning the first major battle of the Civil War. They had pushed the Confederates back, and Southern soldiers were fleeing.

But one Confederate commander would not give up. He was Colonel Thomas Jackson. As southern troops retreated, Jackson ordered his men to remain where they were. They formed a long line and waited for the North to attack.

Jackson's determination gave hope to other Confederate soldiers. General Bernard Bee saw Jackson and cried out, "Look at Jackson's brigade standing like a stone wall! Rally on the Virginians!" Jackson led his men in an attack on Northern soldiers. By the end of the day, the South had won the Battle of First Manassas. Jackson, now called "Stonewall," was made a general and became one of the first military heroes of the Civil War.

pneumonia: a serious disease that causes the lungs to become inflamed and filled with a thick fluid that makes breathing difficult

Thomas "Stonewall" Jackson

William T. Sherman

General William Tecumseh Sherman served under Grant. He was chosen to command the Union's Western armies. Sherman was a good strategist. He was also stubborn. Even under the worst conditions, he refused to quit.

Sherman is most known for his victories at the end of the war. In the fall of 1864 Sherman's troops pushed toward Atlanta. They destroyed farms and buildings on their way. After the Union army captured Atlanta, Sherman's men marched to the Atlantic Ocean. They could not be stopped. On December 21 Sherman sent word to Lincoln that he had taken Savannah, Georgia. His troops' "March to the Sea" showed Confederates that their own army could not protect them. In a few months, the war would end.

strategist: a person who makes a plan for obtaining a specific goal

During the "March to the Sea", the Union army destroyed Southern farms, buildings, and railway routes.

LIFESAVERS

The men and women who fought in Civil War battles were heroes to their families and countrymen. They took great risks to defend their beliefs.

Alexander T. Augusta

Alexander Augusta was a man of many firsts. He was the first commissioned black officer in the United States Army. He was also one of the first black surgeons to serve in battle zones. In order for Augusta to work as a surgeon, he appealed directly to Lincoln.

Alexander Augusta, first commissioned black officer in the United States Army

commissioned: given a military rank

appeal: to request something from someone of authority for a decision

Lincoln allowed Augusta to become a wartime surgeon. But the white doctors did not like him being their boss. Augusta was reassigned to a hospital for free blacks. However, despite the challenges he faced, Augusta inspired many black Americans.

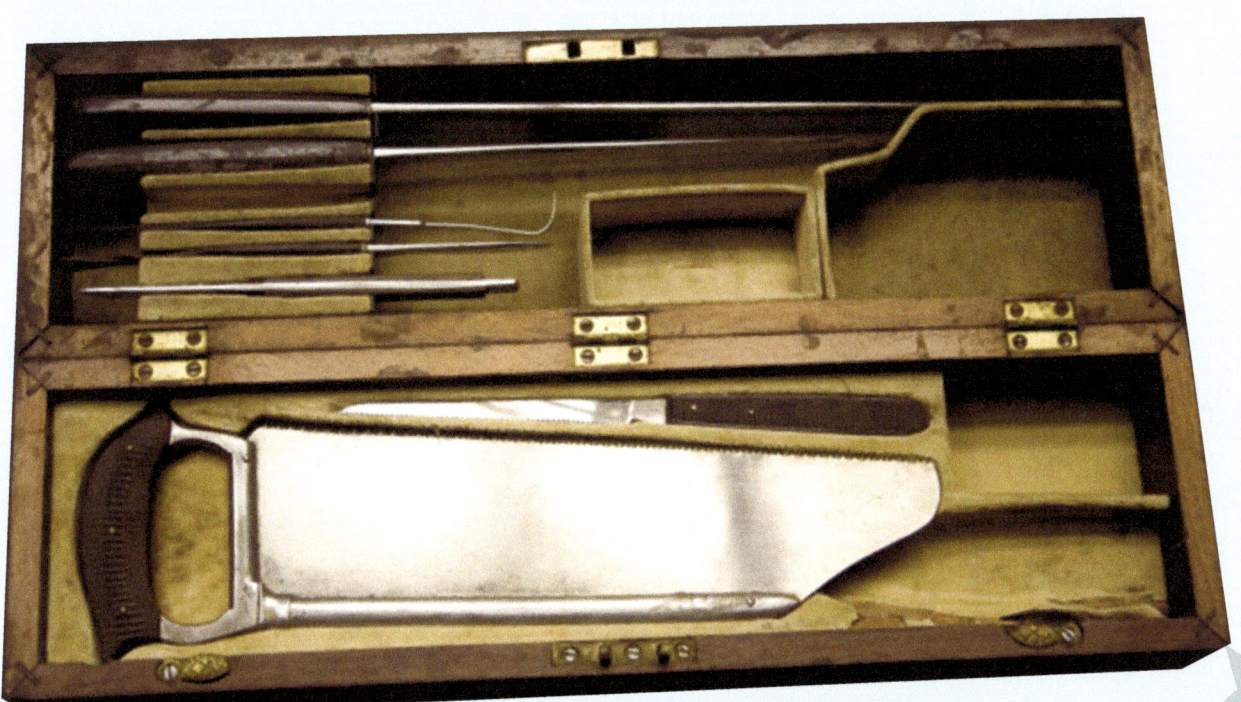

A medical kit from the Civil War era always included a saw for amputating limbs.

Clara Barton

When the Civil War started in 1861, Clara Barton heard the Union army was short on supplies. She wanted to help. Barton collected bandages, medicine, food, and clothes. She delivered supplies directly to the battle sites. Often, she put herself in danger.

Barton gave comfort to the ill and dying. She also nursed many soldiers back to health. Even when she fell ill with typhoid, she returned to the front lines as soon as she could. She did not want to stop helping soldiers. Her service earned her the nickname "Angel of the Battlefield."

Clara Barton started the American Red Cross following her service in the Civil War.

typhoid: a serious infectious disease with symptoms of high fever and diarrhea that sometimes leads to death

Dorothea Dix

Dorothea Dix was not trained as a nurse. Yet, she was appointed superintendent of all female nurses in the Union army. Dix had strict rules for nurses. A woman had to have good character, plain looks, and be more than 30 years old. She couldn't wear colorful clothing, bows, curls, or jewelry. Dix recruited more than 2,000 nurses.

Dorothea Dix

Brave Nurses

Before the Civil War, nurses were mostly men. Women jumped to help during the war. Many nurses thought it was the next best thing to being a soldier.

Most nurses had little or no formal training. Often they did not know how to change a bandage. They quickly learned to give medicine and dress wounds. The hours were long and hard. Nurses often slept on cots in corners of hospitals. They cleaned, fed soldiers, and ordered food and supplies. They wrote letters to soldiers' families.

Only nurses with nerves of steel helped during surgeries. They assisted doctors who operated on soldiers and performed amputations. The women who served at army camps and on the battlefields were heroes of the Civil War. They became known as "angels of mercy."

superintendent: a high-ranking officer who directs the work of an organization

Citizen Heroes

Mary Bowser

Mary Bowser was a freed slave. During the Civil War, she worked as a spy for the Richmond Union Underground. Bowser landed a job as one of Jefferson Davis' servants in the Confederate White House. She was the perfect Union spy because she worked for the Confederate president. No one suspected her, since it was illegal in the South to teach slaves to read.

Bowser carefully listened to Davis' conversations. When she was alone in his study, she read war documents and plans. She gave information to Thomas McGiven, who was the Union spymaster. He was undercover as a baker delivering to the Confederate White House. Bowser wrote messages in code and gave them to McGiven to deliver to Union army leaders.

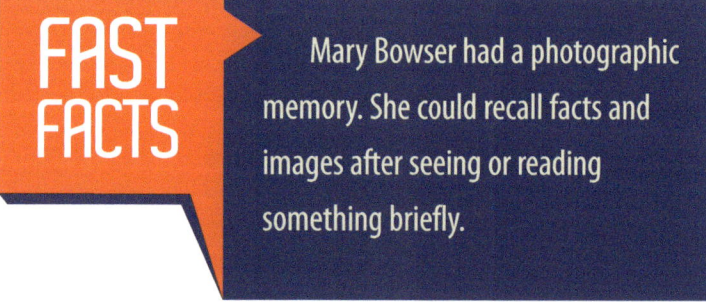

FAST FACTS Mary Bowser had a photographic memory. She could recall facts and images after seeing or reading something briefly.

Women at Work

When the Civil War began, nearly every family was affected in some way. With husbands and brothers away at war, women's lives changed. Some women had to take jobs that were previously considered "men's work."

Women served as clerks and factory workers. They worked the family farm or helped run the family business. Many women volunteered as nurses. Some organized small hospitals and gathered supplies for the troops. Some led the fight against slavery.

A number of women also played key roles in battles. Some gave medical care to wounded soldiers, while others acted as spies. On rare occasions, some women even traveled with their husbands into combat.

Sarah Edmonds pretended to be a man so she could fight for the Union in the Civil War. Her fellow soldiers spoke highly of her even after her disguise was discovered.

Frederick Douglass

One of the best-known abolitionists was Frederick Douglass. During the Civil War, he recruited black men for military service. He wrote a monthly newsletter in which he encouraged black men to join the Union army. Through his efforts, Douglass helped recruit more than 100 free black men, including two of his own sons.

Robert Smalls

Robert Smalls was a slave who co-piloted the Confederate steamboat *Planter*. An all-black crew manned the steamer. On May 12, 1862, the *Planter's* white officers left the boat for the night. Several of Smalls' family members came aboard. Early the next morning, Smalls ordered the crew to take the boat north, out of the harbor in Charleston, South Carolina.

On its way to Union waters, Smalls' boat had to pass many dangerous Confederate blockades. No one stopped the steamer. The *Planter* crew knew the salutes, and it was a well-known boat. From a distance, it was not suspicious. As the boat approached Union waters, the crew raised a white flag. Smalls delivered everyone aboard to safety.

salute: a special hand signal, sign, or greeting

The crew was rewarded with money for delivering the boat to the Union. Smalls met with President Lincoln. Smalls was named captain of the *Planter* and continued to fight for the Union until the end of the Civil War.

Frederick Douglass

Robert Smalls

Harriet Tubman

Harriet Tubman was a runaway slave and a conductor on the Underground Railroad. This network of safe houses helped runaway slaves reach safety in the North. She had a mission to free other slaves. During the Civil War, she worked as a Union scout and spy. In 1863 she led a raid at Combahee Ferry in South Carolina. It resulted in the escape of more than 300 slaves. One Union officer was very impressed by Tubman. He said that she was the only woman, "black or white," to plan and lead a military raid.

Tubman was also a respected field nurse. She was asked by the governor of Massachusetts to work in military camps. She used her knowledge of roots and herbs to treat many injured soldiers.

Harriet Tubman

Elizabeth Van Lew

Elizabeth Van Lew lived in the Confederacy. However, she did not agree with slavery or secession. She risked her life to spy for the Union. Van Lew organized a spy ring. It was called the Richmond Union Underground. Many of the spies were former slaves. They carried secret messages and important documents to the North. Information was hidden in food baskets, hollowed-out eggshells, hooped skirts, and secret compartments in their shoes. In 1864 the Union made her an official federal agent.

Heroes Remembered

Both the North and the South had heroes. They led men into battle, cared for the wounded, and fought for their beliefs. These heroes influenced the events of the Civil War and forever shaped the history of the United States.

Glossary

abolish (uh-BOL-ish)—to put an end to something officially

appeal (uh-PEEL)—to request something from someone of authority for a decision

commissioned (kuh-MI-shund)—given a military rank

Congress (KAHNG-gruhs)—the government body of the United States that makes laws, made up of the Senate and the House of Representatives

emancipation (i-MAN-si-pay-shuhn)—freedom from slavery or control

patriotism (PEY-tree-uh-tiz-uhm)—love for one's country

pneumonia (noo-MOH-nyuh)—a serious disease that causes the lungs to become inflamed and filled with a thick fluid that makes breathing difficult

proclamation (prah-cluh-MAY-shuhn)—a public announcement or statement

salute (suh-LOOT)—a special hand signal, sign, or greeting

secede (si-SEED)—to withdraw formally from a group or an organization, often to form another organization

strategist (STRAT-i-jist)—a person who makes a plan for obtaining a specific goal

superintendent (soo-pur-in-TEN-duhnt)—a high-ranking officer who directs the work of an organization

typhoid (TYE-foid)—a serious infectious disease with symptoms of high fever and diarrhea that sometimes leads to death

Read More

McManus, Lori. *Key People of the Civil War.* Why We Fought, the Civil War. Chicago: Heinemann Library, 2011.

Senior, Kathryn. *You Wouldn't Want to Be a Nurse During the American Civil War!: A Job That's Not for the Squeamish.* You Wouldn't Want to Be. New York: Franklin Watts, 2010.

Yomtov, Nelson. *True Stories of the Civil War.* Stories of War. North Mankato, Minn.: Capstone Press, 2013.

Critical Thinking Using the Common Core

1. What three kinds of heroes are described in this book? Use evidence and quotations from the book to support your answer. List one example for each type of hero. (Key Ideas and Details)

2. Look at the chapter titles and main headings. How is the text organized? Use specific examples. Why do you think this organization helps the reader? (Craft and Structure)

3. Pick one hero in this book. Use other books or Internet sites to learn more about this person. Write one or two paragraphs introducing the person and explaining why he or she is a Civil War hero. Be sure to include evidence from multiple sources. Share what you found out with a partner or a group. (Integration of Knowledge and Ideas)

Internet Sites

FactHound offers a safe, fun way to find Internet sites related to this book. All of the sites on FactHound have been researched by our staff.

Here's all you do:

Visit www.facthound.com

Type in this code: 9781491407202

Check out projects, games, and lots more at www.capstonekids.com

Index

abolition, 4, 8, 9, 26
Antietam, Battle of, 8
Augusta, Alexander T., 20–21

Barton, Clara, 6, 22
Bee, Bernard, 16
Bowser, Mary, 24

Davis, Jefferson, 6, 8, 10, 11, 14, 24
Dix, Dorothea, 6, 23
Douglass, Frederick, 7, 26

Edmonds, Sarah, 25

Grant, Ulysses S., 5, 12–13, 18

Jackson, Thomas "Stonewall," 7, 16, 17

Lee, Robert E., 5, 7, 12, 13, 14, 15
Lincoln, Abraham, 6, 7, 8, 9, 12, 18, 20, 27

March to the Sea, 18, 19
McGiven, Thomas, 24
medical care, 20–21, 22, 23, 25, 28, 29

Sherman, William T., 7, 18
Smalls, Robert, 26–27
spying, 24, 25, 28, 29

Tubman, Harriet, 7, 28

Underground Railroad, 28

Van Lew, Elizabeth, 29